DEPARTMENT OF THE NAVY
HEADQUARTERS UNITED STATES MARINE CORPS
2 NAVY ANNEX
WASHINGTON, DC 20380-1775

I0409670

POLICY FOR PERSONNEL RECOVERY AND REPATRIATION

DEPARTMENT OF THE NAVY
HEADQUARTERS UNITED STATES MARINE CORPS
2 NAVY ANNEX
WASHINGTON, DC 20380-1775

MCO 3460.2
POE
2 Dec 02

MARINE CORPS ORDER 3460.2

From: Commandant of the Marine Corps
To: Distribution List

Subj: POLICY FOR PERSONNEL RECOVERY AND REPATRIATION

Ref: (a) DOD Directive 2310.2 of 22 Dec 00, Personnel Recovery
      (b) DOD Instruction 2310.4 of 21 Nov 00, Repatriation of
          Prisoners of War (POW), Hostages, Peacetime Government
          Detainees and Other Missing or Isolated Personnel
      (c) DOD Directive 1300.7 of 8 Dec 00, Training and Education to
          Support the Code of Conduct (CoC)
      (d) DOD Instruction 1300.21 of 8 Jan 01, Code of Conduct Training
          and Education
      (e) Executive Agent Instruction, Joint Personnel Recovery Agency
          (JPRA), Handling Guidance For Recovered, Returned, and
          Repatriated U.S. Personnel
      (f) CJCSI 3270.01 of 01 Jul 98, Personnel Recovery Within the
          Department of Defense
      (g) DOD Instruction 2310.5 of 31 Jan 00, Accounting for Missing
          Persons
      (h) Title 10 U.S.C. (NOTAL)
      (i) MCO 3460.1A of 11 Jun 90, Training and Education Measures
          Necessary to Support the Code of Conduct
      (j) Joint Pub 3-50.2 of 12 Jul 94, Doctrine for Joint Combat
          Search and Rescue (CSAR)
      (k) Joint Pub 3-50.21 of 31 Dec 94, Joint Tactics, Techniques,
          and Procedures for Combat Search and Rescue
      (l) Joint Pub 3-50.3 of 6 Sep 96, Joint Doctrine for Evasion and
          Recovery
      (m) DOD Instruction 2310.6 of 13 Oct 00, Non-Conventional
          Assisted Recovery in the Department of Defense

Encl: (1) DOD/CJCS-Directed CINC Personnel Recovery Responsibilities
      (2) DOD/CJCS-Directed Secretaries of the Military Departments,
          Services, and CINC USSOCOM Personnel Recovery
          Responsibilities
      (3) Required Minimum Levels of Code of Conduct/SERE Training
      (4) Primary JPRA-sponsored Personnel Recovery Training Available
          to Marines

1. Situation. This Order is published to meet joint requirements
concerning the development of policies for Personnel Recovery (PR),
repatriation, and the establishment of related-training programs as
outlined in the references. The Department of Defense (DOD) policy and
assignment of the executive agent and office of primary responsibility
for PR is contained in references (a) and (b).

a. <u>DOD Policy</u>. Preserving the lives and well-being of U.S. military, DOD civilian, and contract service employees placed in danger of being isolated, beleaguered, detained, captured, or having to evade while participating in a U.S.-sponsored activity or mission is one of the highest priorities of the DOD. The DOD has a moral obligation to protect its personnel, prevent exploitation of its personnel by adversaries, and reduce the potential for captured personnel being used as leverage against the U.S.

b. <u>Principal Staff Assistant/Civilian Advisor to the Secretary of Defense and Office of Primary Responsibility (OPR)</u>. The Assistant Secretary of Defense for International Security Affairs (ASD(ISA)), under the Secretary of Defense for Policy, serves as the principal staff assistant and civilian advisor to the Secretary of Defense and Under Secretary of Defense for Policy on personnel recovery. The ASD(ISA) has designated the Defense Prisoner of War (POW)/Missing Personnel Office (DPMO) as his OPR for personnel recovery.

c. <u>Executive Agent and Office of Primary Responsibility (OPR)</u>. DOD has assigned the Commander United States Joint Forces Command (USJFCOM) as the executive agent for PR, which includes repatriation. The Joint Personnel Recovery Agency (JPRA) is designated as the USJFCOM OPR for repatriation guidance and procedures.

d. <u>U.S. Marine Corps Office of Primary Responsibility (OPR)</u>. CMC assigned Deputy Commandant, Plans, Policies, and Operations (DC PP&O) as the USMC OPR for PR and repatriation matters. DC PP&O in turn assigned the Expeditionary Policies Branch (POE) as the proponent for PR. An officer, whose primary duties are PR, is specifically assigned to the MAGTF/SPECOPS Section (POE-30).

e. <u>Responsibilities</u>. The references contain information and instructions for use by all parties involved in various aspects of PR and repatriation. In addition, they also identify and direct specific responsibilities. Enclosures (1) and (2) outline those DOD/CJCS-directed responsibilities for the combatant commands and the secretaries of the military departments respectively.

2. <u>Mission</u>. To issue the Marine Corps' policy regarding PR and repatriation, and establish requirements for related training.

3. <u>Execution</u>

   a. <u>Commander's Intent and Concept of Operations</u>

      (1) <u>Commander's Intent</u>

         (a) A hallmark of the Marine Corps throughout its history has been the recognized importance of its personnel. The Marine Corps lives by the adage that "Marines Take Care of Their Own". At no time will this be more important than when Marines have been captured, detained, or held hostage by an enemy or other hostile entity. Immediate action will be taken to recover Marines that have been lost in areas of risk due to mishap or hostile action. In the event that immediate recovery is not possible and a Marine is captured or detained, the Marine Corps will closely monitor the efforts of other national assets/organizations working to secure the release of our Marines. The Marine Corps will participate and cooperate in those efforts as required. Once the Marine is returned to U.S. control, the focus will be on attending to the well-being of the returnee in order to facilitate post incident repatriation and timely return to full duty.

(b) Recovery and repatriation may occur in wartime, contingencies, and/or military operations other than war (MOOTW). Repatriation processing will be markedly different for individuals depending on the circumstances and duration of their absence from U.S. control. Some personnel may have spent time in harms' way after some incident/mishap occurs without any contact with enemy personnel or other hostile entities. Some may have been captured and confined in a hostile environment in which they were maltreated, while still others may have been detained for some period of time in a more neutral or benign setting. Commanders will ensure that local procedures are established that allow for the handling of returnees from across this spectrum of experiences.

(c) Recovered personnel may not be limited to USMC personnel. Due to our forward presence, USMC units may encounter returnees from a variety of services, agencies, and/or organizations, including military and civilian personnel. Commanders will ensure close coordination with other services, agencies, and/or organizations in order to return recovered personnel to them for further repatriation efforts.

(d) Commanders will ensure that the appropriate level of code of conduct (COC) training is conducted prior to deployment of personnel to a theater, according to the applicable combatant commander's guidance and in concert with references (c) and (d). When examining the need for higher levels of COC training, an individual's risk of capture and exploitation are the determining factors. The specific identification of "at risk personnel," who require higher levels of training, will be the responsibility of commanders acting in concert with combatant command guidance and that given in this Order.

(2) Concept of Operations

(a) Commanders will develop policies and procedures, in concert with applicable combatant command regulations, this Order, and all applicable references for the recovery and repatriation of Marines and other personnel serving with the Marine Corps. Specifically, commanders will ensure that they and their staffs are familiar with YELLOW RIBBON, which refers to DOD plans and actions related to processing returned U.S. personnel. Under these plans, repatriation is identified as an operational responsibility for the services. There are three phases of repatriation: Phase 1 begins when the returnee first comes under U.S. military control; Phase 2 begins upon arrival at the theater treatment and processing facility; Phase 3 begins when the returnee is transported to a CONUS facility. While a combatant command may initiate Phase 1 repatriation upon recovery of personnel, the services are responsible for tracking the status of their personnel in that phase and then continuing the subsequent phases of the repatriation process as required. References (b) and (e) apply.

   (b) Commanders will ensure that their Marines are trained per guidance contained in references (c) and (d) regarding the duties, responsibilities, and conduct of personnel who have become prisoners of war (POWs), government detainees, or hostages. This will include Survival, Evasion, Resistance, and Escape (SERE) training. Commanders will also ensure that assigned DOD government civilians and contract personnel are trained as required. In particular, commanders will ensure that all deploying personnel have received this training in accordance with the requirements of the gaining combatant command.

   b. Subordinate Element Missions

      (1) Deputy Commandant for Plans, Policies, and Operations

         (a) Per reference (a), act as the Marine Corps' principal member of the Office of the Secretary of Defense (OSD) sponsored Personnel Recovery Advisory Group (PRAG).

         (b) Per references (a) and (f), act as the USMC OPR for all matters pertaining to PR and repatriation activities.

         (c) Per reference (b), coordinate all preparations for processing returned USMC personnel and other personnel serving with the Marine Corps and repatriation-related events with the MARFORs, USJFCOM, and JPRA, in advance, to ensure successful repatriation and debriefing outcome.

      (2) Deputy Commandant for Aviation

         (a) Provide a representative(s) to the OSD-sponsored Personnel Recovery Technology Working Group (PRTWG) and Personnel Recovery Technology Integrated Process Team (PRTIPT).

         (b) Upon request provide a representative with operational expertise to advise the Defense Prisoner of War (POW)/Missing Personnel Office (DPMO) representative at all meetings of the National Search and Rescue Committee.

         (c) Coordinate with appropriate U.S. Navy aviation counterparts to ensure visibility into policies and programs related to personnel recovery that effect the Marine Corps.

      (3) Deputy Commandant for Manpower and Reserve Affairs

         (a) Per reference (g), determine and program joint manning requirements for the JPRA as coordinated with USJFCOM.

(b) Assist the MARFORs with casualty assistance matters pertaining to POWs, hostages, peacetime government detainees, evaders, and other missing personnel, as well as processing and repatriating returned personnel.

(c) In coordination with local casualty assistance offices, be responsible for all contacts with, and assistance to, returnee's next of kin (NOK) and for military and civilian matters applicable to processing their returned personnel. Associated responsibilities include:

<u>1</u> Establish procedures to notify NOK when personnel are released from captivity or otherwise recovered and to keep the families of POWs, hostages, peacetime government detainees, evaders, and other missing personnel not released from captivity or recovered from isolation, advised of processing activities and releasable information on status determination.

<u>2</u> Per ref (b), provide applicable advisories to NOK including information on anticipated YELLOW RIBBON procedures, the arrival of returned personnel, and processing schedules.

<u>3</u> Provide additional support, as directed, to facilitate orderly, expeditious, and considerate processing of returned personnel and ensure efficient operation of all related activities.

(d) Assist the MARFORs, as required, in planning public affairs (PA) assistance for the returnee and his/her family, consistent with the principles of information while respecting individual privacy.

(e) To the extent allowed by applicable law and regulations, ensure that funding is available to cover the costs associated with repatriating individual returnees, to include military personnel, DOD civilians, and DOD contract employees. For DOD civilians and contractors, these costs include billeting, transportation, security, medical treatment determined to be necessary, and other military service-directed activities associated with the repatriation process.

(f) Administer the Marine Corps program regarding accounting for missing persons covered by reference (h), sections 1501-1513. Reference (g) also applies.

(4) <u>Commanding General, Training and Education Command</u>

(a) Validate and accredit all USMC Personnel Recovery and Repatriation training to ensure it conforms to the policies in references (c) and (d). This will include instruction in the methods of survival, evasion, resistance, and escape under varying degrees of hostile exploitation. Specifically:

<u>1</u> In concert with references (c), (d), and (i), ensure that entry-level COC training (level A) is conducted for all Marines entering service.

   <u>2</u> Assist commanders in the conduct of level B COC/SERE training as required by combatant commanders. Facilitate the distribution of training materials to commanders as required.

   <u>3</u> In coordination with DC PP&O, DC AVN, and the MARFORs, work with the JPRA, the U.S. Navy's SERE Schools, and other services, organizations, and agencies as required, to determine quota requirements and ensure attendance of Marines in high-risk-of-capture (SERE level C) training courses. Ensure adequate funding is available to support the quota plan.

   <u>4</u> In coordination with DC PP&O and the MARFORs, determine quota requirements for PR-related training at JPRA, U.S. Navy, and other accredited courses. Ensure adequate funding is available to support the quota plan.

   <u>5</u> In concert with references (c), (d), and this Order, ensure common training standards are developed for COC training programs.

   <u>6</u> Periodically review and update reference (i), ensuring that it reflects the most current Marine Corps training and education measures in support of the COC.

  (b) In concert with references (j), (k), and (l), ensure common training standards are developed for Tactical Recovery of Aircraft and Personnel (TRAP), and peacetime search and rescue (SAR) missions.

  (5) <u>Director, Intelligence</u>

  (a) Per reference (a), provide a representative to attend periodic Department of Defense's PR Intelligence Steering Group meetings, as required.

  (b) Provide oversight and direction for the conduct of returnee debriefings. Per references (b), (e), and (l), returnee debriefing procedures will take into consideration the following:

   <u>1</u> Once safety, security, and immediate medical concerns have been addressed, intelligence personnel will conduct tactical debriefings. These debriefings will be limited strictly to perishable tactical information the returnee may possess, such as time-sensitive information on U.S. personnel last seen alive in a POW camp system, but still in an unaccounted for status.

   <u>2</u> Intelligence personnel will conduct more detailed debriefings during later phases of repatriation as deemed necessary. Initiation of such briefings will be coordinated with attending medical personnel to ensure returnees are ready and fully capable of participating.

        3 Returnee debriefings shall be obtained under an express written promise of confidentiality. Debriefings shall be treated as privileged information under the provisions of reference (h), section 1506(d)(1), are the property of the DOD, and shall not be released to the public. DD Form 2810, Promise of Confidentiality, shall be used to inform returnees that debriefings will remain confidential to the extent authorized by law. Prior to starting the debriefing process, the returnee shall be given an opportunity to sign this form.

        (6) Staff Judge Advocate to the Commandant of the Marine Corps. Assist the MARFORs, as required, in ensuring sufficient legal personnel are available to advise returned personnel and their families of their legal rights and benefits, and to serve as the focal point on matters pertaining to their personal legal challenges.

        (7) Medical Officer of the Marine Corps/Health Services

        (a) Provide overall guidance and instruction on the medical aspects of the repatriation process.

        (b) Assist the MARFORs, as required, with ensuring that applicable medical arrangements associated with returnee processing are in place before repatriation, consistent with applicable law and regulations.
        (c) Ensure that adequate numbers of SERE-trained psychologists are assigned to support psychological and mental health portions of repatriation debriefings.

        (8) Chaplain of the Marine Corps

        (a) Develop and maintain awareness of the DOD YELLOW RIBBON Plan among chaplains; the sensitivities of issues surrounding POWs, hostages, peacetime governmental detainees, evaders, and other missing personnel; as well as rehabilitation and readjustment challenges that returned personnel and their families may experience.

        (b) Consistent with applicable laws and regulations, ensure sufficient Chaplains and supporting religious personnel are available at CONUS and OCONUS processing locations to meet the spiritual needs of returned personnel and their families.

        (c) In coordination with M&RA, and the MARFORs, ensure chaplains are available and prepared to assist in conveying potentially distressing news to returned personnel and their families, as well as the families of POWs, hostages, peacetime governmental detainees, evaders, and other missing personnel.

        (9) Commander, Marine Forces Atlantic; Commander, Marine Forces Pacific; and Commander, Marine Forces Reserve

        (a) Training

<u>1</u> In accordance with the guidance of the gaining combatant command(s), references (c), (d), (i), and this Order, ensure that the appropriate level of COC training is conducted for all personnel. Specifically:

<u>a</u> Ensure that annual Level A refresher training is conducted for all personnel.

<u>b</u> Identify moderate-risk-of-capture/exploitation personnel and ensure that they attend Level B training. Also, ensure refresher/continuation/additional training is conducted for this level, as required by the gaining combatant command, prior to deployment and/or participation in contingency operations.

<u>c</u> Identify high-risk-of-capture/exploitation personnel and ensure that they attend Level C SERE training. Also, ensure refresher/continuation/additional training is conducted for this level, as required by the gaining Combatant Command, prior to deployment and/or participation in contingency operations.

<u>d</u> Ensure that assigned DOD civilians and contract personnel receive applicable levels of COC/SERE training commensurate with combatant commander's requirements prior to deployment to, or assignment at, overseas locations. As with military members; a civilian's billet assignment, access to sensitive knowledge and information, and, in particular, their risk of capture and exploitability, are the determining factors in deciding on the need for, and level of, required training.

<u>e</u> Ensure that completion of COC/SERE training is entered into MCTFS. Updates should be entered to reflect completion of required refresher/continuation training as well.

<u>2</u> Conduct periodic inspections of unit SERE/COC and TRAP/SAR training programs to ensure they conform to applicable orders and directives.

<u>3</u> Identify personnel involved in PR activities in their command or personnel currently serving, or who will serve, to oversee PR activities in their command and ensure that they attend available training. Enclosure (4) outlines the primary JPRA-sponsored training courses available to Marine Corps personnel.

(b) <u>Recovery</u>

<u>1</u> In concert with references (a), (f), (j), (k), (l), (m), and applicable combatant command regulations, ensure that all operational plans address the recovery of personnel. Organize, train, and equip appropriate forces for TRAP missions in support of operations, exercises, and contingencies. Coordinate with TECOM on training standards. Ensure that such recovery plans and missions are periodically exercised and evaluated.

<u>2</u> In concert with reference (k) and applicable combatant command regulations, plans and procedures, establish USMC Rescue Coordination Centers (RCCs) during exercises and operations as required. Be prepared to augment U.S. Navy Rescue Coordination Teams (RCTs) with USMC personnel, as required. Be prepared to augment theater Joint Search and Rescue Centers (JSRC) with USMC personnel as required. Ensure that adequate numbers of personnel are trained in the plans, procedures, and architecture of PR within the applicable theater(s).

<u>3</u> Be prepared to assign forces, units, and equipment to joint recovery operations and to lead such operations when directed. References (j), (k), and (l) apply.

<u>4</u> Assess capabilities and identify any shortfalls in the areas of PR and repatriation to the USMC PR OPR (PP&O).

<u>5</u> Assign Marines to non-conventional assisted recovery (NAR) operations as required. Train personnel on NAR procedures as required. References (h), (i), (j), and (m) apply.

(c) <u>Repatriation</u>

<u>1</u> Commanders of USMC units and/or personnel making initial contact with returnees shall attend to their immediate safety, security, and well being. As the situation dictates, they will ensure that returnees are evacuated as quickly as possible to a secure location. Recovered personnel should be immediately assessed and treated by available medical personnel as necessary.

<u>2</u> Ensure subordinate commanders have established procedures for the repatriation of personnel in accordance with references (b) and (e). Be especially cognizant of the following:

<u>a</u> Ensure that adequate debriefing facilities and logistical support are available in CONUS and that they meet minimum requirements as set forth in emerging USJFCOM guidance.

<u>b</u> Ensure supporting plans and directives are prepared and issued before repatriation of personnel. Coordinate each repatriation event with DC PP&O in advance to ensure successful repatriation and debriefing outcome.

<u>c</u> Designate specific CONUS installations as potential processing locations and task commanders of designated installations to develop YELLOW RIBBON contingency plans.

<u>3</u> Appoint, in writing, a YELLOW RIBBON processing team chief (O-6) at each installation in CONUS designated as a potential processing location. Report this information to the USMC PR OPR (PP&O) as required.

<u>a</u> The processing team chief shall be the central coordinator and point of contact for all processing preparations and

activities at that installation for all military, DOD civilian, and DOD contract employee returnees.

b The processing team chief shall not be encumbered with other specific responsibilities such as medical treatment, debriefing, or normal duties when YELLOW RIBBON contingency plans are implemented.

c The processing team chief will assist the installation commander in developing plans to prevent unauthorized access to the returnee(s) and family members during the repatriation process. The processing team chief will develop access rosters with installation commanders, as required, to ensure only authorized personnel have access to processing areas.

4 Commanders, in coordination with JPRA representatives and key medical staff, shall control access to the returnee, paying special attention to arrival, hospital stay, debriefing, and time spent at personnel processing facilities.

5 In coordination with local medical staffs, and the office of the Medical Officer of the Marine Corps, ensure adequate medical arrangements associated with returnee processing are in place before repatriation.

6 In coordination with local PA offices, and the HQMC Public Affairs Office, plan PA assistance for the returnee and his/her family consistent with the principles of information while respecting individual privacy.

7 Ensure sufficient chaplains and supporting religious personnel are available at both CONUS and OCONUS processing locations to meet the spiritual needs of returned personnel and their families.

8 In coordination with the M&RA's Casualty Assistance Branch, develop casualty assistance procedures pertaining to POWs, hostages, peacetime government detainees, evaders, and other missing personnel and for processing and repatriating returned personnel.

c. Coordinating Instructions

(1) Training

(a) There are three levels of COC/SERE training (A, B, and C). In addition, within Levels B and C, there are three orientations, Wartime (POW), Peacetime Government Detention, and Hostage/Terrorist Detention. The levels focus the training on the service member's understanding of the 6 articles found in the COC, from an entry level understanding at level A to a greater and more in-depth understanding of the articles and of SERE techniques in levels B and C. The three differing orientations are aimed at teaching personnel how to behave depending on their status and the identity and intentions of their captors. Per reference (c), the levels of training are defined as follows:

        <u>1</u> Level A is the minimum level of understanding for all members of the Armed Forces to be taught during the entry level training of all personnel.

        <u>a</u> Level A is taught to all Marines during recruit training and officer candidate training. This level of training consists of classroom instruction aimed at familiarizing personnel with the articles of the COC with an emphasis on their interpretation and use in wartime situations.

        <u>b</u> Annual Level A refresher training is a requirement for all Marines.

        <u>2</u> Level B is the minimum level of understanding for military service members whose military jobs, specialties, or assignments entail moderate risk of capture and exploitation. As a minimum, the following categories of personnel shall receive level B training at least once in their careers: members of ground combat units, security forces, and anyone in the immediate vicinity of the forward edge of the battle area or the forward line of troops. Training shall be conducted for such service members as soon as they assume a duty that makes them eligible. Level B training consists of classroom training only, and will follow guidance published by the JPRA.

        <u>a</u> While combatant command guidance may identify additional requirements for Level B training, the Marine Corps specifically requires this level for the following, as a minimum: all personnel assigned to Combat, Combat Support, and Security Force units. This includes, but is not limited to, the Marine Divisions and all fleet anti-terrorist security companies and overseas security force companies. This requirement will include all Combat Service Support and U.S. Navy personnel attached to these combat, combat support, and security force units. Naval aviators, naval flight officers, and enlisted aircrews should also receive Level B Peacetime Government Detention and Hostage training until such time as the U.S. Navy SERE Schools fully develop and implement a Level C peacetime training program in addition to their current wartime program. Commanders have the discretion to identify and train such other personnel at Level B, as they deem necessary. See enclosure (3).

        <u>b</u> This training will be accomplished at the unit level, and must incorporate, at a minimum, training videos produced by the JPRA and distributed by TECOM. This videotaped instruction is organized into 3 series categorized by detention type: wartime (WT); peacetime government detention (PGD); and peacetime hostage (PTH). There are classified and unclassified tapes in each series. Personnel with a secret or higher security clearance must view both the unclassified and classified tapes in order to be credited with completion of Level B training. Personnel who do not possess a security clearance need only view all of the unclassified tapes to be credited with completion. The processing of personnel for security clearances for the sole purpose of viewing the classified tapes in

these series is unnecessary and prohibited. When recording this
training in the Marine Corps Total Force System (MCTFS), the Unit Diary
entry should specify whether a Marine completed the classified or
unclassified version of the training using the appropriate service
school code (SSC) as follows:

<u>SSC</u> <u>Description</u>
XJN Peacetime/Government Detention (Unclassified)
XJP Peacetime/Government Detention (Classified)
XJR Peacetime/Hostage Detention (Unclassified)
XJS Peacetime/Hostage Detention (Classified)
XJT Wartime Detention (Unclassified)
XJV Wartime Detention (Classified)

        <u>3</u> Level C is the minimum level of understanding for
military service members whose military jobs, specialties, or
assignments entail significant or high risk of capture and
exploitation. This group of personnel should not be limited to those
whose position, rank, seniority, or exposure to top secret or higher
classified information makes them vulnerable to greater-than-average
exploitation efforts by a captor. As a minimum, the following
categories of personnel shall receive formal Level C training at least
once in their careers: combat aircrews, special operations forces
(e.g., Navy special warfare combat swimmers and special boat units,
Army special forces and rangers, Marine Corps force reconnaissance
units, Air Force special tactics teams, and psychological operations
units) and military attaches. Training shall be conducted for such
service members as soon as they assume duties or responsibilities that
make them eligible.

        <u>a</u> While combatant command guidance may identify
additional requirements for Level C training, the Marine Corps
specifically requires this level for the following, as a minimum:
personnel who routinely over-fly hostile territory or operate forward
of the main battle area. This includes, but is not limited to, naval
aviators; naval flight officers; enlisted aircrews; force
reconnaissance and reconnaissance battalion personnel assigned to
reconnaissance teams; radio battalion personnel assigned to radio
reconnaissance platoons; scout snipers; personnel assigned to firepower
control teams; personnel assigned to counter-intelligence/human
exploitation teams and personnel assigned to Surveillance Sensor
Operator platoons. Commanders have the discretion to identify and
train such other personnel at Level C as they deem necessary, but
should carefully consider an individual's billet assignment, sensitive
knowledge, and their risk of capture and exploitation in determining
whether or not they actually require this level of training. See
enclosure (3).

        <u>b</u> Level C training consists of academic classroom,
laboratory, and field/hands-on training. Level C training courses must
be approved and accredited by JPRA, and will only be conducted at
service SERE schools or other locations approved by JPRA.

(b) The appropriate level of COC training will be conducted for all personnel, as required by the gaining combatant command, whether they are deploying individually or by unit, and whether they are military, DOD civilian, or contractor.

(c) Per references (c) and (d), the commanders of the combatant commands shall determine the level of training required of personnel entering the command's area of operation. As described in reference (b), the degree of knowledge military members require concerning the COC is dictated by the service member's susceptibility to capture, the amount of sensitive information the service member has, and the potential captor's or detaining power's likely assessment of the Service member's usefulness and value in terms of exploitability. The combatant commanders' interpretation of this may result in requirements for training that are more stringent than the minimums described above in paragraph 3c(1)(a) 2 and 3. In such cases, the combatant commanders' guidance will take priority.

(d) The Marine Corps is responsible for identifying and qualifying COC and SERE training specialists. The JPRA is responsible for accrediting these trainers. For example, since Marines attend the Navy's SERE schools, there are Marine detachments assigned to each of them that provide accredited instructors and other personnel to augment their staffs. Repatriation issues and concepts are addressed in JPRA PR resident courses, and training conducted in the field, by designated JPRA Repatriation subject matter experts during contingency operations. Repatriation-specific training is limited to the JPRA Debriefers Course. See reference (b).

(e) It is critical to record an individual's completion of COC training so that their status can immediately be determined. Recording such information also ensures that supplementary and/or refresher training is provided when required. As an individual completes various levels of COC training, and receives refresher/continuation training, this will be entered into the MCTFS.

(2) Recovery

(a) Reference (g) requires that the services "Perform CSAR in support of own operations consistent with capabilities and assigned functions and IAW the requirements of the supported combatant commander." The Marine Corps meets this requirement through the training and employment of forces for the Tactical Recovery of Aircraft and Personnel (TRAP) mission. TRAP provides the MAGTF both a self-recovery capability and may also be executed in support of other forces/elements during joint operations. TRAP is coordinated and initiated by local commanders per their standard operating procedures and theater recovery plans in concert with guidance contained in references (j), (k), and (l). TRAP can be further described as follows:

1 TRAP is an implied task for all MAGTF operations.

          2 Forces are trained and designated but not dedicated solely to the TRAP Mission alone.

          3 TRAP missions emphasize detailed planning. The planning process reduces uncertainty and confusion during mission execution.

          a The TRAP concept of operations is concise and developed in conformity to Theater SOPs with an emphasis on complementing other force capabilities.

          b A TRAP contingency plan is developed for each assault. TRAP force packages are designated and contingency planning is conducted.

          c The above factors and prior staff training facilitate rapid final planning pursuant to mission execution as each event unfolds.

          4 TRAP differs from Combat Search and Rescue (CSAR) in that: there is no extended search phase in TRAP; the location of the survivor must be known within 1 nautical mile and there must be reasonable assurance that the survivor is alive and not in imminent danger of capture; forces are trained and designated, but not dedicated, to the mission; and there is an emphasis on combat power and deliberate execution in accomplishing the recovery. TRAP is a proven and viable form of recovery that complements other CSAR capabilities.

          a In addition to personnel recovery, TRAP missions emphasize aircraft & equipment recovery, repair, and destruction as required.

          b The TRAP mission is planned and executed as a form of tactical raid and involves thorough maneuver, fire support, and contingency planning. The TRAP force is capable of securing and holding a site until rescue, recovery, repair, and/or destruction work is completed. The force is task-organized to accomplish all of these tasks as required.

          c All of the MAGTF's forces, assets, and capabilities are considered. Planning and task-organization provide the flexibility to adapt to changing tactical situations.

          (b) The joint forces commander has primary authority and responsibility for personnel recovery in support of U.S. forces within the AOR per references (a) and (g). Reference (g) also specifically requires joint force commanders to establish a Joint Search and Rescue Center (JSRC), or its equivalent, to coordinate and integrate PR planning and operations capabilities within the AOR. The Joint Force Commander may task a component commander to designate the component Rescue Coordination Center (RCC) as the JSRC. References (h), (i), and (j) apply.

       <u>1</u> The JSRC is the primary theater search and rescue facility for planning, coordinating, and executing search and rescue and combat search and rescue operations within the geographical area assigned to the joint force. The JSRC is the joint force commander's focal point for personnel recovery operations and integrates all theater operations to support and recover isolated personnel.

         <u>a</u> Historically, many joint force commanders have tasked the Joint Forces Air Component Commander (JFACC) with designating the component RCC as the JSRC also. The JFACC's JSRC/RCC is normally a subordinate organization within the Joint Air Operations Center (JAOC).

         <u>b</u> The joint force commander and/or component commander may call upon other service commanders to augment the JSRC.

       <u>2</u> The RCC (called the Rescue Coordination Team (RCT) by the U.S. Navy) is the primary component search and rescue facility for coordinating and controlling search and rescue and/or combat search and rescue operations. Personnel of a single service or component normally operate this facility unilaterally. The Tactical Air Command Center (TACC), when established, normally assumes the duties as the Marine Corps' RCC.

         <u>a</u> The service/component RCC must have the means (staffing, communications, and authority) to conduct planning, coordinate with the JAOC, JSRC, and other service/component rescue centers, and execute and control personnel recovery operations per combatant command plans and procedures.

         <u>b</u> A service/component RCC must be prepared to act as the lead RCC in the event that the CJTF/JAOC/JSRC assigns a joint recovery mission to that service/component.

      (c) Upon successfully recovering an individual, the recovering force will immediately treat any life-threatening injuries and coordinate with the JSRC to deliver the individual into the planned repatriation process as soon as possible.

    (3) <u>Repatriation</u>

      (a) Per reference (e), returnees should be transported to an evaluation site or "safe area" as soon as possible. This can be any location, which is estimated to meet the criterion of "safe area" in terms of the returnee's perception. The following should be accomplished at the safe area:

       <u>1</u> The returnee(s) will be met by a unit command representative and receive necessary medical treatment. Ideally, a SERE psychologist/psychiatrist from the local command, working in concert with a JPRA SME, will be immediately available to conduct a screening of the returnee(s). Per ref (b), a SERE psychologist/psychiatrist should be a part of any repatriation team and

remain with the returnee(s) throughout the repatriation process. After the conduct of this screening, the unit commander will be briefed concerning the psychological condition of the returnee(s). The commander will weigh the psychological assessment to determine how and when the returnee(s) will continue with debriefing and repatriation. Note: JPRA, as the DOD Executive Agent's OPR for repatriation, has the responsibility to assist the services in repatriation. Reference (c) identifies JPRA's role to "oversee all debriefing activities". Debriefing activities include intelligence, PR (Operational and SERE), and other government agencies (OGA) debriefings.

  <u>2</u> Once medically cleared, intelligence personnel will obtain critical, time-sensitive, operational information from returnee(s) before they continue processing. Reference (1) applies.

  (b) Per reference (b), Marine sponsor(s) will be assigned to USMC returnees to respond to questions and provide assistance during repatriation processing. In addition to unit command representatives, a sponsor will be present to meet the returnee(s) and remain with him/her until such time as the commander determines their assistance is no longer required. The sponsor will provide moral support only, and not be assigned duties, such as administrative or operational debriefing. This individual should obviously have a favorable existing rapport with the returnee and, if possible, be identified well prior to the returnee's release from detention/captivity.

  (c) Each returnee's situation will be different and handling procedures will vary depending on the individual circumstances.

  <u>1</u> If the returnee is evaluated by medical personnel, and determined to be psychologically injured in some way, the handling process will accommodate the appropriate level and duration of treatment and/or rehabilitation. Attempts to debrief the individual to gain information may be inappropriate and have to be suspended, deferred, and/or cancelled. The desire of all repatriation efforts is to prepare the returnee for transition back to their desired status. Commanders will closely coordinate decisions concerning the schedule for such a transition.

  <u>2</u> Commanders will work closely with appropriate medical authorities to determine the schedule and procedures used in the repatriation of individuals who have suffered significant physical injuries during confinement/detainment.

  <u>3</u> If the returnee is not found either psychologically and/or physically injured, the handling process should focus on how best to prepare the returnee to transition back to full duty. This is accomplished while gaining necessary medical, operational, and other specific information about his/her particular situation.

  (d) Assigned personnel will accompany returnees during the handling process and assist them as required.

<u>1</u> If the returnee desires, every effort will be made to facilitate contact with a family member by phone as soon as practical.

<u>2</u> The returnee will be ensured privacy from non-critical DOD individuals and organizations, the press, and other outside agencies or individuals.

<u>3</u> The sponsor, or other designated USMC representative, will be present to discuss issues related to his/her detention/captivity. Initially, this should be limited to time-sensitive items, such as other detainees left behind, those who died in captivity, etc.

(4) <u>Follow-on Repatriation Processing</u>

(a) Once the returnee completes medical/psychological assessment and debriefing he/she will proceed depending on their unique situation.

<u>1</u> The individual may be returned to full duty status without further action. The individual may be encouraged to take a period of leave by his/her local command as is deemed appropriate.

<u>2</u> The individual may require local medical treatment for some period of time prior to a period of leave/family visit and final return to his/her unit.

<u>3</u> Some circumstances may warrant the movement of the individual to a specified location for family reunion, more intelligence debriefings, more detailed discussion of the individual's detention/captivity experiences, and/or required follow-up medical care. The desired outcome is that upon completion of stateside medical care and debriefings, the Marine will return to full duty.

(b) Commanders will maintain visibility concerning the disposition of returnees.

4. <u>Administration and Logistics</u>

a. <u>Administration</u>

(1) <u>Joint Personnel Recovery Training</u>. Commanders will ensure designated personnel receive appropriate training in the areas of Joint Personnel Recovery and theater-specific Personnel Recovery architecture and procedures prior to deployment. Enclosure (4) outlines the primary JPRA-sponsored training courses available to Marine Corps personnel.

(2) <u>Repatriation Processing Team Chiefs</u>. Each installation in CONUS designated as a potential processing location is required to appoint, in writing, a YELLOW RIBBON processing team chief (O-6) and report this information to the USMC PR OPR (HQMC PP&O, POE - 30, ATTN: Personnel Recovery Officer). An updated report will be required annually at the end of each fiscal year.

b. Logistics

(1) Level B SERE Tape/CD Series. The initial issues of the Level B SERE Tape/CD Training Series have been provided to the Services by the JPRA. All subsequent changes and updates necessitating new versioning and reissue will be initiated by the JPRA. Local reproduction of these training series is authorized in order to replace worn out, damaged, or lost materials. Such reproduction, however, should be closely controlled so as to account for all sets of the training materials distributed and to facilitate the subsequent collection and destruction of complete series in the event that new versions are issued by JPRA. To that end, accountability/control will be maintained for all sets of the Tape/CD Training Series distributed. Individual tapes/CDs shall not be reproduced and distributed separately.

(2) Inquiries concerning the Level B SERE Tape/CD Training Series and all other Code of Conduct/SERE-related training should be directed to Training and Education Command (TECOM), Ground Training Branch, MCCDC, Quantico, VA.

5. Command and Signal

a. Command. This policy will be effective upon signature.

b. Signal. This Order is applicable to the Marine Corps Total Force.

K. B. KUKLOK
Deputy Commandant for
Plans, Policies, and Operations
Acting

DISTRIBUTION: PCN 10203321000

Copy to: 7000144/8145001 (1)

DOD/CJCS-Directed CINC Personnel Recovery Responsibilities

Para	Subpara	DoDD 2310.2 "Personnel Recovery", 22 December 2000
		(13 Total)
5.14.		The Commanders of the Combatant Commands are responsible for planning and executing personnel recovery operations within their area of responsibility and shall:
	5.14.1.	Establish and maintain an office of primary responsibility for personnel recovery operations, training, doctrine, support, and execution and notify DPMO, USJFCOM, and JPRA of the office designated.
	5.14.2.	Establish and maintain command procedures and programs for personnel recovery.
	5.14.3.	Include personnel recovery as an integral part of all operational planning and training. This shall include the full spectrum of recovery operations (including repatriation) and include training of recovery forces as well as those at high-risk-of-capture (e.g., aviators and special operations personnel).
	5.14.4.	Identify requirements for and shortfalls in personnel recovery capabilities.
	5.14.5.	Submit operational intelligence requirements for personnel recovery to the J-2, USJFCOM.
	5.14.6.	Identify all personnel recovery requirements annually. This shall include, but is not limited to, non-conventional assisted recovery requirements.
	5.14.7.	In coordination with the Services and USSOCOM, develop standards for determining personnel requiring mid- and high-risk-of-capture training (Levels B and C). Categories of personnel which should be considered for high-risk-of-capture training (Level C) include, but are not limited to: Special Operations Forces, aviators, and other personnel who operate deep within or over hostile territory or whose duties make them especially vulnerable to exploitation by enemy forces if captured.
	5.14.8.	Support requests for personnel recovery assistance from allied, coalition, and paramilitary forces, when directed by the National Command Authorities.
	5.14.9.	Support JPRA, and establish clear, direct, and expeditious lines of communication between the command and JPRA, and with DPMO on policy matters for personnel recovery.
	5.14.10.	Develop theater admission requirements for DoD civilian and contractor service personnel as required. Include SERE training requirements for DoD civilians and contract personnel operating in-theater in accordance with the "risk-of-capture" environment in which they will work.
	5.14.11.	Comply with provisions of reference (g) (DoD Instruction 2310.5, "Accounting for Missing Persons,") for determining the status of missing persons and for the systematic, comprehensive, and timely collection, analysis, review, dissemination, and periodic update of information related to such persons.

ENCLOSURE (1)

	5.14.12.	Coordinate all international search and rescue agreements through ASD(ISA) via DPMO. Provide a list of existing agreements and a summary of each to DPMO.
	5.14.13.	When deemed necessary, provide Flag Officer representation as a principal member of the PRAG (or appropriate representation as a supporting member or observer of the PRAG) and applicable representation to the PRTWG in accordance with subparagraphs 5.2.9.2. and 5.5.4.2., respectively, of this Directive. In the absence of a Flag Officer, a representative from the Combatant Command should attend the PRAG.

		CJCSI 3270.01, "PR Within the Department of Defense", 1 July 1998
Para	Subpara	(13 Total)
2.e.		In accordance with reference a (DoDD 2310.2 "Personnel Recovery"), geographic combatant commanders will:
	(1)	Establish an OPR for PR doctrine and execution.
	(2)	Develop and publish an integrated PR program IAW DoD policy and joint doctrine that supports DoD activities and operations within the AOR. The program will incorporate both conventional and unconventional assisted recovery (UAR) capabilities.
	(3)	Identify intelligence and other requirements to support theater PR programs and plans. This includes, but is not limited to, PR information and aids. Forward requirements through established procedures to include the PR/OPR for inclusion in the appropriate DOD intelligence requirement and SERE production documents.
	(3)(a)	Material classified SECRET
	(3)(b)	Material classified SECRET
	(4)	Coordinate with the appropriate Service(s) and the PR/OPR to ensure personnel being repatriated are properly debriefed. Provide analysis to the PR/OPR, DPMO, Services, other combatant commanders, and Defense agencies concerning the effectiveness and appriateness of respective PR support.
	(5)	Material classified CONFIDENTIAL
	(6)	Material classified SECRET
	(7)	Material classified SECRET
	(8)	Revise theater admission requirements for DoD civilian and contractor service personnel.
	(9)	Material classified CONFIDENTIAL
	(10)	In accordance with reference l (CJCSI 3110.01A, "JSCP", 15 Nov 1995), maintain a list of unconventional warfare areas and state the priority and desired readiness date of each. Areas may be designated as Evasion and Recovery (E&R), guerrilla warfare (GW), or subversion areas, or as multiple purpose areas when planning two or more types of operations. Provide a capability statement for each type of activity specifically identified within any multipurpose area.
	(11)	Material classified SECRET

	(12)	Identify PR capabilities, requirements, and deficiencies to the Services.
	(13)	Establish a Joint Search and Rescue Center (JSRC), or equivalent, to coordinate and integrate PR planning and operations capabilities with the AOR.

		DoDI 2310.5, "Accounting for Missing Persons", 31 January 2000
Para	Subpara	**(2 Total)**
5.6.		The Commanders of the Combatant Commands shall comply with the instructions contained herein.
5.7.		All DoD Components shall, in response to written requests made by the president of the board, which is convened pursuant to the Missing Persons Act (reference (b)), release information to the board president in accordance with the procedures contained at section E5.6.

		DoDD 1300.7, "Training and Education to Support the Code of Conduct (CoC), 8 December 2000
Para	Subpara	**(2 Total)**
4.5.		The Commander, United States Joint Forces Command, as the DoD Executive Agent for the CoC, shall oversee and monitor CoC training, planning, and support to the DoD Components. USJFCOM has designated the Joint Personnel Recovery Agency (JPRA) as its office of primary responsibility for DoD-wide CoC training and education measures, as stated in DoD Directive 2310.2 (reference (f)). USJFCOM shall ensure that clear, direct, and expeditious lines of communication exist among JPRA, DPMO, and the Services on policy matters for CoC.
4.6.		The Commanders of the Combatant Commands, in coordination with the Chairman of the Joint Chiefs of Staff, shall designate the level of training (i.e., Level A, B, or C) that personnel operating in the area of operation of a Combatant Command shall have before deploying into theater and identify those requirements to the respective Services.

		DoDI 1300.21, Code of Conduct Training and Education, 8 January 2001
Para	Subpara	**(3 Total)**
4.4.		The Commanders of the Combatant Commands shall:

	4.4.1.	Designate the level of training (i.e., Level A, B or C) personnel operating in the command's area of operation must have prior to deployment to theater, and communicate these requirements to the respective Services. CoC training needs should be identified for wartime requirements as well as for areas considered high risk due to terrorist activities and areas with the likely potential for detention of members of the Armed Forces by foreign governments for the purpose of exploitation. The Commanders of the Combatant Commands must determine who is considered high-risk-of-capture and exploitation for the purpose of CoC training. During war and operations other than war, personnel operating beyond the forward line of troops (e.g. all aviators, Special Operations Forces, long-range reconnaissance patrol members) are clearly in more danger than others of becoming prisoners of war. Combat forces generally require higher-level CoC training than support forces. As such, the commands must identify their requirements precisely, and they and the Services must train them to the applicable level.
	4.4.2.	Determine CoC continuation training requirements for personnel identified to operate in the command's area of operations.
	4.4.3.	Require all personnel to receive CoC training commensurate with their risk-of-capture level prior to deployment to the command's area of operations.
		DoDI 2310.4, "Repatriation of Prisoners of War (POW), Hostages, Peacetime Government Detainees and Other Missing or Isolated Personnel", 21 November 2000
Para	Subpara	**(8 Total)**
5.7.		The Commanders of the Combatant Commands shall:
	5.7.1.	Be responsible for the returnee's initial processing.
	5.7.2.	Develop applicable command plans in coordination with JPRA to support this Instruction.
	5.7.3.	Review the supporting plans and preparations of the Component commanders and subordinate units to ensure they conform with the spirit and intent of this Instruction, including medical and spiritual care, initial debriefing, and administration of the comfort and welfare of the returnee.
	5.7.4.	Designate OCONUS installations with treatment and processing facilities for initial returnee medical evaluation, stabilization, and debriefing.
	5.7.5.	Coordinate with the United States Air Force for returnee aeromedical evacuation.
	5.7.6	Ensure procedures exist to notify promptly the Military Service OPRs, DPMO, JPRA, the Military Service Casualty Offices, and the Chief of Chaplains Offices of the initial release and of subsequent information, including medical information, on returned U.S. personnel.

ENCLOSURE (1)

	5.7.7	Ensure Component commanders provide required collateral support to assist in returning U.S. personnel.
	5.7.8	Develop plans and procedures to take custody of returned personnel from IO or NGO representatives as soon as possible after release.

		DoDI 2310.6, "Non-conventional Assisted Recovery in the Department of Defense", October 13, 2000
Para	Subpara	(9 Total)
5.6.		The Commanders in Chief of the Geographic Combatant Commands shall:
	5.6.1.	Designate a NAR OPR.
	5.6.2.	Include NAR planning in operations and exercises and develop requirements for NAR to complement the commands' other personnel recovery capabilities and support theater operations plans.
	5.6.3.	Forward NAR requirements to the Chairman of the Joint Chiefs of Staff for validation, coordination and sourcing if component commands do not possess the required trained personnel or other assets needed to plan and successfully execute NAR.
	5.6.4.	Identify and plan for NAR requirements annually.
	5.6.5.	Establish, prioritize, and manage theater NAR requirements, engaging all potential supporting and operational elements in the developmental process.
	5.6.6.	Establish clear and expeditious lines of communication with the Chairman of the Joint Chiefs of Staff, USJFCOM, USSOCOM, and DPMO on policy matters for NAR.
	5.6.7.	Plan, coordinate, and prepare to execute NAR with the assistance of Joint Personnel Recovery Agency (JPRA), and Defense and other Government Agencies, in accordance with Combatant Command policies, procedures, joint doctrine and accepted tactics, techniques, and procedures.
	5.6.8.	Establish command and control measures to ensure integration of NAR procedures into Combatant Command personnel recovery plans and procedures, and Joint Search and Rescue Center operations.
	5.6.9.	Coordinate with USSOCOM for all command NAR requirements for SOF personnel, tactics, training, funding and equipment.

ENCLOSURE (1)

DoD/CJCS-Directed Secretaries of the Military Departments, Services, and CINC USSOCOM Personnel Recovery Responsibilities

Para	Subpara	DoDD 2310.2 "Personnel Recovery", 22 December 2000
		(14 Total)
5.11.		The Secretaries of the Military Departments and the Commander in Chief, United States Special Operations Command, shall:
	5.11.1.	Ensure that personnel recovery capabilities (facilities, equipment, training, personnel, etc.) are developed, programmed, and budgeted to accommodate the personnel recovery requirements of the Services and the Combatant Commands.
	5.11.2.	Establish Service and USSOCOM offices of primary responsibility for coordinating all personnel recovery matters and notify DPMO, USJFCOM and JPRA of the office designated.
	5.11.3.	Provide results of Service and USSOCOM inspection programs regarding personnel recovery matters to DPMO, USJFCOM, and JPRA.
	5.11.4.	Determine and program for joint manning requirements for JPRA in accordance with reference (f) [CJCSM 1600.01, Joint Manpower Program Procedures], and as coordinated, with USCINCJFCOM.
	5.11.5.	Provide appropriate level Code of Conduct training, as directed in reference (e) [DoD Directive 1300.7, "Training and Education Measures Necessary to Support the Code of Conduct], to those forces designated and assigned to a Combatant Commander.
	5.11.5.1.	Conduct applicable pre-deployment refresher training prior to deployment of personnel participating in contingency operations.
	5.11.5.2.	In coordination with the Combatant Commands, develop standards for determining personnel requiring mid- and high-risk-of-capture training (Levels B and C). Categories of personnel that should be considered for high-risk-of-capture training (Level C) include, but are not limited to: Special Operations Forces, aviators, and other personnel who operate deep within or over hostile territory or whose duties make them especially vulnerable to exploitation by enemy forces if captured.
	5.11.5.3.	Ensure DoD civilians and contract personnel receive applicable levels of SERE training commensurate with theater admission and Combatant Command requirements prior to deployment to overseas locations.
	5.11.6.	Establish Service and USSOCOM repatriation plans incorporating guidance from applicable DoD Instructions, and from Combatant Commands and JPRA.
	5.11.7.	Ensure policies and procedures are in place to identify and track personnel who have been trained or are experienced in personnel recovery operations and command, control, computers, and intelligence. This will ensure commanders can request and receive personnel qualified to support personnel recovery requirements.

Para	Subpara	
	5.11.8.	Comply with provisions of reference (g) [DoD Instruction 2310.5, "Accounting for Missing Persons"] for determining the status of missing persons, and for the systematic, comprehensive, and timely collection, analysis, review, dissemination, and periodic update of information related to such persons.
	5.11.9.	Provide Flag Officer representation to the PRAG and applicable representation to the PRTWG in accordance with subparagraphs 5.2.9.2. And 5.4.4.2., respectively, of this Directive.
	5.11.10.	Provide representation with operational expertise to advise the DPMO representative at all meetings of the National Search and Rescue Committee, on the request of the Director, DPMO.
5.12.		The Secretary of the Air Force shall continue to provide administrative support for financial management, manpower, and personnel services for JPRA. The U.S. Air Force shall fund JPRA through the Future Years Defense Program via the DoD Planning, Programming, and Budgeting Process.
		CJCSI 3270.01, "PR Within the Department of Defense", 1 July 1998
Para	Subpara	**(5 Total)**
2.d.		The Services and USSOCOM will:
	(1)	Designate an OPR/point of contact (POC) that coordinates all aspects of PR.
	(2)	Perform CSAR in support of own operations consistent with capabilities and assigned functions and IAW the requirements of the supported combatant commander.
	(3)	Facilitate effective SERE, Code of Conduct, and CSAR training; categorize Service/USSOCOM members by risk of capture during peace, war, and MOOTW as determined by combatant commanders. Identify training shortfalls and deficiencies through appropriate channels and include the PR/OPR as an addressee.
	(4)	Provide Service/USSOCOM members appropriate equipment and training to facilitate their successful return to US control in event of isolation. The PR/OPR is responsible for advising the Services about appropriate equipment and training.
	(5)	This material classified CONFIDENTIAL
		DoDI 2310.5, "Accounting for Missing Persons", 31 January 2000
Para	Subpara	**(4 Total)**
5.5.		The Secretaries of the Military Departments shall:
	5.5.1.	Administer Service programs regarding missing persons covered by reference (b) [Sections 1501-1513 of title 10, United States Code] consistent with the procedures in section 6., below.

ENCLOSURE (2)

MCO 3460.2

	5.5.3.	Address any recommendations for procedural changes in this Instruction to the Under Secretary of Defense for Policy, ATTN: DPMO.
5.6.		All DoD Components shall, in response to written requests made by the president of a board, which is convened pursuant to the Missing Persons Act (reference (b)), release information to the board president in accordance with the procedures contained at section E5.6.
		DoDI 1300.7, "Training and Education to Support the Code of Conduct (CoC), 8 December 2000
Para	Subpara	**(3 Total)**
4.3.		The Secretaries of the Military Departments shall:
	4.3.1.	Conduct CoC training validated and accredited by the Services.
	4.3.2.	Train Service personnel to the levels required by the Commanders of the Combatant Commands (paragraph 4.6., below) before deployment of personnel to the theater.
	4.3.3.	Forward for resolution by DPMO doctrinal or training issues that are not resolved in coordination with the Commander, United States Joint Forces Command (USJFCOM).
		DoDI 1300.21, Code of Conduct Training and Education, 8 January 2001
Para	Subpara	**(7 Total)**
5.2.		The Secretaries of the Military Departments shall:
	5.2.1.	Train all personnel in the applicable level of CoC training as identified by the Commanders of the Combatant Commands. Training related to the CoC shall be conducted at three levels for the following categories of personnel:
	5.2.1.1.	Level A. Minimum level of understanding for all members of the Armed Forces, to be imparted during entry training of all personnel.
	5.2.1.2.	Level B. Minimum level of understanding for Military Service members whose military jobs, specialties, or assignments entail moderate risk of capture and exploitation. As a minimum, the following categories of personnel shall receive Level B training at least once in their careers: members of ground combat units, security forces for high threat targets, and anyone in the immediate vicinity of the Forward Edge of Battle Area or the Forward Line of Troops. Training shall be conducted for such Service members as soon as they assume a duty that makes them eligible.

Para	Subpara	
	5.2.1.3.	Level C. Minimum level of understanding for Military Service members whose military jobs, specialties, or assignments entail a significant or high risk of capture and exploitation. This group of personnel should not be limited to those whose position, rank, seniority, or exposure to Top Secret or higher classified information make them vulnerable to greater-than-average exploitation efforts by a captor. As a minimum the following categories of personnel shall receive formal Level C training at least once in their careers: combat aircrews, special operations forces (e.g., Navy special warfare combat swimmers and Special Boat Units, Army Special Forces and Rangers, Marine Corps Force Reconnaissance units, Air Force Special Tactics teams, and psychological operations units) and military attaches. Training shall be conducted for such Service members as soon as they assume duties or responsibilities that make them eligible.
	5.2.2.	Validate and accredit all Service CoC training and ensure it conforms with the policies in DoDD 1300.7 (reference (a)) and training guidance in this Instruction.
	5.2.3.	Employ qualified Service instructors and material approved for all CoC training to ensure that all personnel receive applicable knowledge prescribed in enclosures 2 and 3.
	5.2.4.	Use existing Military Service inspection programs to evaluate CoC training programs related to CoC to ensure they meet the requirements this Instruction establishes. Ensure that the Military Services provide inspection results to DPMO and JPRA within 30 days of the close of each calendar year.
		DoDI 2310.4, "Repatriation of Prinsoners of War (POW), Hostages, Peacetime Government Detainees and Other Missing or Isolated Personnel", 21 November 2000
Para	Subpara	**(34 Total)**
5.4.		The Secretaries of Military Departments shall:
	5.4.1.	Designate an OPR in each Military Service staff to coordinate all repatriation activities of the respective Military Service.
	5.4.2.	Coordinate all preparations for processing returned DoD personnel with USJFCOM, the DoD executive agent for personnel recovery (of which repatriation is a subset), and USJFCOM shall inform DPMO of the same. Coordination shall be in accordance with the provisions of this Instruction.
	5.4.3.	Ensure that adequate debriefing facilities and logistical support are available in CONUS and that they meet minimum requirements USJFCOM identifies.

ENCLOSURE (2)

	5.4.4.	Ensure supporting plans and directives are prepared and issued before the repatriation of personnel. Since history indicates that each repatriation scenario is unique, coordinate requirements of each repatriation event with USJFCOM in advance to ensure a successful repatriation and debriefing outcome.
	5.4.5.	Designate specific CONUS installations as potential processing locations and task commanders of designated installations to develop YELLOW RIBBON contingency plans. The Military Services shall:
	5.4.5.1.	Appoint, on orders, a YELLOW RIBBON Processing Team Chief (O-6) at each military installation in CONUS designated as a potential processing location.
	5.4.5.1.1.	The Processing Team Chief shall be the central coordinator and point of contact for all processing preparations and activities at that installation.
	5.4.5.1.2.	The Processing Team Chief shall not be encumbered with other specific responsibilities such as medical treatment, debriefing responsibilities, or normal duties when YELLOW RIBBON contingency plans are implemented.
	5.4.5.1.3.	The Processing Team Chief shall assist the installation commander to develop plans to prevent unauthorized access to the returnee and family members during the repatriation process. Installation commanders must control access to the installation to prevent unauthorized individuals from interfering with the processing schedule and the privacy of the returnee and family members. Many well-intentioned and curious individuals of all ranks and offices will desire access to the returnee. The returnee's command authority, in coordination with JPRA, and when indicated, key medical staff, shall control access to the returnee, paying special attention to arrival, the hospital stay, debriefing, and time spent at personnel processing facilities.
	5.4.5.1.4.	The Processing Team Chief should develop and provide access rosters to installation commanders, as required, to ensure only authorized personnel have access to processing areas.
	5.4.5.1.5.	In the event a single (i.e., only one) military returnee is processed at a civilian facility, an O-6 from the military member's Military Service, ideally from the member's home station, shall be appointed as Processing Team Chief. If more than one military returnee is processed at a civilian facility, the Processing Team Chief shall be appointed from the Military Service of the senior military person being processed.
	5.4.5.1.6.	Like their military counterparts, returned DoD civilians and DoD contractor employees shall come under the purview of the Processing Team Chief.
	5.4.5.2.	Maintain current names, ranks, duty telephone numbers, and home telephone numbers of YELLOW RIBBON Processing Team Chiefs.

	5.4.5.3.	Provide additional support, as directed, to facilitate orderly, expeditious, and considerate processing of returned DoD personnel and ensure efficient operation of all related activities.
	5.4.5.4.	Plan PA assistance for the returnee and his or her family consistent with the Principles of Information while respecting individual privacy.
	5.4.5.5.	Arrange prompt dispatch of each returnee's military or civilian record to the correct CONUS processing location when required.
	5.4.5.6.	Augment and support YELLOW RIBBON processing centers to accomplish required personnel actions.
	5.4.5.7.	In coordination with the respective Military Service Surgeon General Offices, ensure applicable medical arrangements associated with returnee processing are in place before repatriation. For these matters, the Military Service Surgeon General Offices shall, consistent with applicable law and regulations:
	5.4.5.7.1.	Provide overall guidance and instructions on medical aspects of the repatriation process.
	5.4.5.7.3	Identify and train Survival, Evasion, Resistance, and Escape (SERE) psychologists with applicable specialties to support psychological and mental health portions of debriefings.
	5.4.5.8.	Consistent with applicable law and regulations, ensure sufficient legal personnel are available to advise returned personnel and their families of their legal rights and benefits, and to serve as focal point on matters pertaining to their personal legal challenges.
	5.4.5.9.	Consistent with applicable law and regulations, ensure sufficient Chaplains and supporting religious personnel are available at the CONUS and outside continental United States (OCONUS) processing locations to meet the spiritual needs of returned personnel and their families. For these matters, the Military Service Chaplain Offices, in coordination with the respective Military Service Casualty Offices, will normally:
	5.4.5.9.1.	Develop and maintain awareness of the YELLOW RIBBON Plan among Chaplains; the sensitivities of issues surrounding POWs, hostages, peacetime governmental detainees, evaders and other missing personnel; as well as rehabilitation and readjustment challenges that returned personnel and their families may experience.
	5.4.5.9.2.	Ensure Chaplains are available and prepared to assist in conveying potentially personally distressing news to returned personnel and their families, as well as the families of POWs, hostages, peacetime governmental detainees, evaders and other missing personnel who do not return.
	5.4.5.9.3.	Augment, as necessary, CONUS Chaplain staffs so returned personnel and family members, regardless of faith, have the opportunity for religious ministration and personal counseling of their choice.

ENCLOSURE (2)

	5.4.5.10.	Military Service OPRs shall maintain a list of designated installations, processing team chiefs, and contact information with copies provided to the Chairman of the Joint Chiefs of Staff, DPMO, and JPRA.
	5.4.6.	Be responsible for all contacts with and assistance to returnee's NOK (use NOK definition found in Title 10 U.S.C., paragraph 1513(4), reference (b)), and for military or civilian matters applicable to processing their returned personnel. The Military Service Personnel Offices will normally authorize their respective Casualty Offices to task and accomplish the following:
	5.4.6.1.	Establish procedures to notify NOK promptly when personnel are released from captivity or otherwise recovered, and to keep the families of POWs, hostages, peacetime governmental detainees, evaders, and other missing personnel not released from captivity or recovered from isolation advised of processing activities and releasable information on status determination.
	5.4.6.2.	Provide applicable advisories to NOK including information on anticipated YELLOW RIBBON procedures, the arrival of returned personnel, and processing schedules.
	5.4.6.3.	Consistent with applicable law and regulations, transport authorized family members to CONUS or OCONUS processing locations according to this Instruction.
	5.4.7.	Develop procedures to support the return of U.S. personnel who have been released by their captors to IO or NGO representatives.
	5.4.8.	Ensure the respective Military Service PA Offices coordinate their efforts through the office of the Assistant Secretary of Defense for Public Affairs.
	5.4.9.	To the extent allowed by applicable law and regulations, fund costs associated with repatriating individual Military Service returnees, to include active duty military personnel, DoD civilians, and DoD contractor employees (e.g., the Army pays costs associated with repatriating soldiers and Department of the Army civilians and contractors; the Navy pays costs associated with repatriating sailors and Department of the Navy civilians and contractors). For DoD civilians and contractors, these costs include billeting, transportation, security, medical treatment determined to be necessary, and other Military Service-directed activities associated with the repatriation process, to the extent allowed by applicable law and regulations.
5.5.		The Secretary of the Air Force shall, to the extent allowed by law and applicable regulations, ensure returnees are provided transportation, to include aeromedical evacuation if necessary, from OCONUS and in CONUS, and ensure expeditious transport of returnee's NOK to the respective processing facility.

		DoDI 2310.6, "Non-conventional Assisted Recovery in the Department of Defense", October 13, 2000
Para	Subpara	(5 Total)
5.4.		The Secretaries of the Military Departments shall train personnel, develop and procure equipment, that meets the requirements for NAR identified the Commanders of the Combatant Commands.
5.8.		The Commander in Chief, United States Special Operations Command under reference (d) [Sections 167 and 1501 of Title 10, United States Code] shall:
	5.8.1.	Develop SOF strategy, doctrine, tactics, techniques and procedures for NAR.
	5.8.2.	Monitor the preparedness of SOF assigned to commands other than USSOCOM to plan and execute NAR.
	5.8.3.	Prepare program recommendations and budget proposals for SOF supporting NAR.
	5.8.4.	Develop and acquire special operations peculiar equipment, material, supplies, and services to support NAR.

ENCLOSURE (2)

REQUIRED MINIMUM LEVELS OF CODE OF CONDUCT/SERE TRAINING

ELEMENT/UNIT	TRAINING LEVEL/PRIORITY			NOTES
	WT	PGD	PTH	
Command Element				
MEF Command Element	A	A	A	1
MEF Headquarters Group (MHG)	A	A	A	1
Comm Bn	A	A	A	1,2
Intel Bn	A	A	A	1,2
HET Personnel	C	B/C	B/C	3
Surveillance Sensor Operators	C	B/C	B/C	3
Radio Bn	A	A	A	1,2
Radio Recon Personnel	C	B/C	B/C	3
Force Recon Co	B	B	B	1
Recon Team Personnel	C	B/C	B/C	3
ANGLICO/MLE	B	B	B	1,2
Firepower Control Team Personnel	C	B/C	B/C	3
Civil Affairs Group	A	A	A	1
Civil Affairs Dets	B	B	B	1
Ground Combat Element				
Div HQ Bn	A	A	A	1
Infantry Regt/Bn	B	B	B	1
STA Plts (Scout Snipers)	C	B/C	B/C	3
Arty Regt/Bn	B	B	B	1
Recon Bn/Co	B	B	B	1
Recon Team Personnel	C	B/C	B/C	3
Tank Bn	B	B	B	1
AA Bn	B	B	B	1
LAR Bn	B	B	B	1
Combat Engr Bn	B	B	B	1
Small Craft Company	B	B	B	1
Aviation Combat Element				
MAW HQ/MWHS	A	A	A	1
MACG HQ	A	A	A	1
MTACS	A	A	A	1
MWCS	A	A	A	1
MACS	A	A	A	1
MASS	A	A	A	1
LAAD	B	B	B	1
MAG HQ (VF/VA & VH)	A	A	A	1
MALS (F/W & R/W)	A	A	A	1
VMA	C	B/C	B/C	3,4
VMFA	C	B/C	B/C	3,4
VMFA(AW)	C	B/C	B/C	3,4
VMAQ	C	B/C	B/C	3,4
VMGR	C	B/C	B/C	3,4
VMU	A	A	A	1
HMLA	C	B/C	B/C	3,4
HMM	C	B/C	B/C	3,4
HMH	C	B/C	B/C	3,4
VMM	C	B/C	B/C	3,4
MWSG HQ/H&HS	A	A	A	1
MWSS (F/W & R/W)	A	A	A	1

ENCLOSURE (3)

1

ELEMENT/UNIT		TRAINING LEVEL/PRIORITY			NOTES
		WT	PGD	PTH	
Combat Service Support Element					
FSSG H&S Bn		A	A	A	1,2
Medical Bn		A	A	A	1,2
Dental Bn		A	A	A	1,2
Supply Bn		A	A	A	1,2
Support Bn		A	A	A	1,2
Maintenance Bn		A	A	A	1,2
Transportation Spt Bn		A	A	A	1,2
Engineer Spt Bn		A	A	A	1,2
Security Forces					
Marine Corps Security Force Battalion		A	A	A	1
Overseas Security Force Co		B	B	B	1
FAST Co.		B	B	B	1
Marine Security Guard Battalion		A	A	A	1
MSG Co/Det		B	B	B	1

Legend:

WT - Wartime Detention (POW)

PGD - Peacetime Government Detention

PTH - Peacetime Hostage Detention

Definitions:

Level A - The minimum level of understanding for all members of the Armed Forces, to be taught during entry training of all personnel.

Level B - Minimum level of understanding for military service members whose military jobs, specialties, or assignments entail moderate risk of capture and exploitation. As a minimum, the following categories of personnel shall receive Level B training: members of ground combat units, security forces for high threat targets, and anyone in the immediate vicinity of the Forward Edge of the Battle Area or the Forward Line of Troops.

Level C - Minimum level of understanding for Military Service members whose military jobs, specialties, or assignments entail a significant risk of capture and exploitation. Categories of personnel that should be considered for High-Risk-of-Capture training include, but are not limited to: Special Operations Forces, aviators, and other personnel who operate deep within, or over, hostile territory or whose duties make them especially vulnerable to exploitation by enemy forces if captured.

Risk of Capture - The degree of possibility for capture or detention in a Wartime, Peacetime Governmental or Hostage/Terrorist situation.

High-Risk-of-Capture Personnel (HRC) - U.S. personnel that operate deep within or over hostile territory or whose duties make them especially vulnerable to exploitation, if captured.

Moderate-Risk-of-Capture Personnel (MRC) - U.S. personnel that operate in/over hostile territory; in proximity to enemy activity; provide physical security for high threat targets or whose duties make them vulnerable to exploitation.

Low-Risk-of-Capture Personnel (LRC) - U.S. personnel that are under only a remote threat of hostile activity or exploitation.

ENCLOSURE (3)

Notes:

. Commanders have the discretion to require a higher level of training than the minimums listed here for any personnel as they deem necessary. In such cases Commanders should decide on the need for a higher level of training on a case-by-case basis based on an individual's risk of capture and exploitation.

. Level B training will be given to personnel who are routinely attached to the Ground Combat Element, or whose duties require them to operate in the vicinity of the FEBA/FLOT, or whose duties and knowledge make them exploitable.

. All USMC personnel that require Level C training will attend the Wartime Program as currently taught by the USN SERE Schools. Those personnel will receive Level B Peacetime Governmental Detention and Hostage training until the USN SERE Schools' Level C Peacetime Detention and Hostage Survival (PDAHS) training program is fully developed and implemented.

. Level B/C training requirements pertain to those personnel functioning as pilots and aircrew to include personnel assigned to aircrew status as a collateral duty such as aerial observers and gunners). Level A is the required minimum for all other personnel.

Primary JPRA-Sponsored Personnel Recovery Training Available to Marines

1. PR 101, Introduction to Personnel Recovery Course.

    a. Purpose: This entry-level course is designed to expose students to DoD's joint personnel recovery (PR) roles and missions as they are currently defined by joint doctrine.

    b. Target Population: The course targets active duty, reserve, and civilian personnel in Grades E4 to O5, or civilian equivalent, who are involved in PR activities in their command. Marines that will find this course relevant are those assigned to units and organizations that plan, conduct, and/or support Tactical Recovery of Aircraft and Personnel (TRAP) missions or that will function as the service/component Rescue Coordination Center (RCC) when deployed to a theater of operations. These may include, but are not limited to, personnel assigned to personnel recovery duties in the Tactical Air Command Center (TACC), personnel assigned to the MEU(SOC) staff and/or to the Ground and Air Combat Element staffs.

    c. Length: 3 days. Offered as a resident course and Mobile Training Team (MTT) delivered course.

    d. Prerequisites: A current Secret Security Clearance.

    e. Syllabus: The course touches on a number of areas including the DoD PR System, categories of DoD recovery, service PR capabilities and limitations, and PR command and control architecture. PR 101 is not a tactical level course. The intent is to expose all service members to the PR arena from the strategic and operational levels of war perspective. Course curriculum includes PR terms and definitions, roles and responsibilities, service organization and missions, the role of the Air Operations Center, PR information dissemination tools, and Joint Search and Rescue Center (JSRC) and Rescue Coordination Center (RCC) operations. The course also examines the importance of supporting functions such as intelligence, communications, SERE, and Life Support. Throughout the course, lessons learned from WWII to Kosovo are used to illustrate the time-tested principals of successful recovery operations.

    f. Course Availability and Scheduling:

        (1) Though subject to change, PR 101 is normally offered in residence 5 times per year at JPRA facilities in Virginia and through MTT-delivered instruction during October and March. Quotas for the resident classes and requests for MTT support are handled by JPRA on a first-come-first-served basis. Training and Education Command, Ground Training Branch will submit a consolidated request for quotas and MTT support for all Marine Corps units/elements as required. Due to facility limitations JPRA must normally limit the class size to 20 students total. A list of class dates will be published annually by separate message.

ENCLOSURE (4)

1

(2) Quotas for the resident classes must be requested through Training and Education Command, Ground Training Branch via phone, FAX, e-mail, or message at least 30 days prior to the course start date.

(3) Requests for PR-101 MTT support must be submitted to Training and Education Command, Ground Training Branch via phone, FAX, e-mail, or message. Requests for MTT support in October must be received by 15 July. The finalized MTT schedule will be published by JPRA by 31 August. Requests for MTT support in March must be received by 15 November. The finalized MTT schedule will be published by JPRA by 15 January. The requesting organization must coordinate a secure facility for Secret-level presentations and verify clearances of all attendees. The MTT staff will allow a class size commensurate with whatever the secure facility chosen by the organization requesting the training can accommodate.

2. PR 301, Personnel Recovery Plans and Operations Course.

a. Purpose: To educate designated theater and component staff officers and non-commissioned officers to oversee the development, management, implementation, and execution of an integrated PR architecture. It also prepares theater and component personnel serving in supporting roles to facilitate successful PR planning and operations.

b. Target Population: The course targets active duty, reserve, and civilian personnel in grades E-7 to O-6, or civilian equivalent, who are currently serving or who will serve to oversee PR activities in their command and personnel who support or may support PR efforts in their command. Marines that will find this course relevant are those assigned to units and organizations that plan, conduct, and/or support Tactical Recovery of Aircraft and Personnel (TRAP) missions or that will function as the service/component Rescue Coordination Center (RCC) when deployed to a theater of operations. These may include, but are not limited to, personnel assigned to personnel recovery duties in the Tactical Air Command Center (TACC), and personnel assigned to the MEU(SOC) staff and/or to the Ground and Air Combat Element staffs.

c. Length: 10 days. Resident course only.

d. Prerequisites: In order to attend PR 301 you must meet one of the following criteria:

(1) Successful completion of PR 101, Introduction to Personnel Recovery; or

(2) Have an immediate operational need, which precludes attending PR 101 first. JPRA J7 must approve PR 101 waivers. Waiver requests will be submitted to Training and Education Command, Ground Training Branch at the same time as the quota request. See paragraph 3.b.(2) below. The waiver request must include a brief narrative explaining the operational requirement that precludes the person(s)

ENCLOSURE (4)

from attending PR 101 prior to attending PR 301.

      (3) A current Secret Security Clearance is required.

   e. Syllabus: The academic program emphasizes a hands-on approach and focuses on joint PR doctrine, information, principles, and concepts. The curriculum integrates real world scenarios, problem-centered practical exercises, and critical analysis. The emphasis is on how to apply the processes to effect successful recovery operations. The course is designed using a building block approach, comprising of successive modules, with integrated practical exercises, and a final comprehensive culmination exercise. Modules include: PR Planning Cycle – Recovery Force Considerations; PR Planning Cycle – PR Command and Control; Repatriation Planning; JSRC/RCC Overview; and PR Operations Cycle – Mission Management.

   f. Course Availability and Scheduling:

      (1) Though subject to change, PR 301 is normally offered in residence 7 times per year at JPRA facilities in Virginia. The Marine Corps is assigned one dedicated quota per class. Additional quotas may be available upon request. JPRA limits the class size to 17 students total. Training and Education Command, Ground Training Branch will submit a consolidated request for quotas for all Marine Corps units/elements as required. A list of class dates will be published annually by separate message.

      (2) Quotas must be requested through Training and Education Command, Ground Training Branch via phone, FAX, e-mail, or message at least 45 days prior to the course start date. Requests for the one dedicated USMC quota are on a first-come-first-serve basis with priority to deploying forces. Additional quotas will be sought, as requested, but cannot be guaranteed.

ENCLOSURE (4)

3

www.ingramcontent.com/pod-product-compliance
Lightning Source LLC
Chambersburg PA
CBHW080634290526
45790CB00007B/3057